LAW OF ATTRACTION

HANDBOOK

LAW OF ATTRACTION
HANDBOOK

Revealing the Secrets to Manifest
Your Desires Instantly to Success

The Invisible Paths

Aiman A. Al-Maimani

iUniverse, Inc.
New York Bloomington Shanghai

Law of Attraction handbook
Revealing the Secrets to Manifest Your Desires Instantly to Success

iUniverse books may be ordered through booksellers or by contacting:

iUniverse
1663 Liberty Drive
Bloomington, IN 47403
www.iuniverse.com
1-800-Authors (1-800-288-4677)

Because of the dynamic nature of the Internet, any Web addresses or links contained in this book may have changed since publication and may no longer be valid.

The information, ideas, and suggestions in this book are not intended as a substitute for professional advice. Before following any suggestions contained in this book, you should consult your personal physician or mental health professional. Neither the author nor the publisher shall be liable or responsible for any loss or damage allegedly arising as a consequence of your use or application of any information or suggestions in this book.

ISBN: 978-0-595-42974-5 (pbk)
ISBN: 978-0-595-71594-7 (cloth)
ISBN: 978-0-595-87315-9 (ebk)

Printed in the United States of America

To my parents … from my heart to yours.
I am delighted to dedicate this book to you.

Contents

Acknowledgments

My sincere gratitude goes to my wife and life partner, Arwah, for her support and encouragement to have the focus to complete this book.

Also, I wish to thank the following people for their excellent work and support. My editor, Kathy Smith, whose hard work and intuitive way with words has helped make this book a reality. My book cover and Web site designer, Bevin Stephenson, whose creativity and light brings color and richness to everything she does. The staff at my publisher, iUniverse, for their kind and caring support throughout this project.

And to each of my life teachers. Thank you for your special wisdom and insights: Michael J. Losier, Jack Canfield, Chunyi Lin, Esther Hicks, Jerry Hicks, Rhonda Byrne, Ehryck F. Gilmore, Dr. Norman Vincent Peale, Sandra Anne Taylor, Dr. Salah Alrashed, Dr. Ibrahim Elfiky, Dr. Stephen R.

Covey, James Arthur Ray, Bob Doyle, Shakti Gawain, Anne Marie Evers, Joe Vitale, Brian Tracy, and Philip C. McGraw.

Preface

In the twenty-first century, many people face a fast-paced and hectic day-to-day lifestyle. They often struggle to find a comfortable balance between work and home in their lives, all the while reaching for what often seems to be an elusive dream or goal.

Now I'm not necessarily talking about dreams of becoming a millionaire or a famous actor. I'm talking about the everyday dreams and goals people have. Some people aspire to move one more step up the corporate ladder; some want to change careers and work in a field they've always wanted to be in; some want to learn to sing; and others want better relationships with their families and friends. No matter what the dream or goal, it's in our nature as humans to strive to get there, to bring into reality that which we want to achieve.

Yet somehow the dreams seem elusive, no matter what a person tries to do. Sometimes people can be inhibited by their personal life histories—you know, repeating negative and unproductive thoughts and behaviors—or they're stuck in a pattern of people-pleasing and feel compelled to live their lives the way others want and expect them to.

So, with these challenges, how can people know where and how to start to connect with themselves again and finally find the path that leads them to their ultimate goals?

The first thing to do is to accept responsibility for where you are right now and to remove any blame you have put on others for where you find yourself currently in your life.

I know it's much easier for some of us to blame others, to blame the rules, or to claim that we do not have the resources to attain what we want. It's also much easier to say we do not have the money and the time to work on our desires. Surprisingly, we often take an "I'm the innocent one" stance and blame our troubles on everything or everyone around us.

Pause for a moment and ask yourself, "Is this going to get me anywhere?"

True, there are circumstances—things—that happen to us that are out of our control. But what we *do* with what happens to us and, more importantly, how we *react and act* determines our future.

For instance, imagine this scenario:

One day, you're running late for an important meeting at work. You madly rush out of the house and jump into your car, and just as you're backing down the driveway, you spot the garbage truck coming your way. As you wait for it to pass, it stalls right behind you and blocks you.

You have two choices here, one positive and one negative. You can get out of the car and start yelling at the garbage truck driver, throw your car keys angrily onto the ground, stomp up and down, and scream obscenities into the air.

Or …

You can quietly and calmly ask the driver what the problem is, if you can help, and how long he/she thinks it will take until he/she can move the vehicle. Then you can quickly call your office and tell them of the delay and that you'll be there as soon as you possibly can.

In either case, you *know* that truck is going to move eventually—yes, it's true that it could be in the next five minutes or in the next five hours, but it *will* move. All you have to do is decide what action you want to take to get the best results for yourself and everyone involved.

So …

The outcome of the event will still be the same—it's just how *you* decide to deal with it that makes all the difference.

The reason I'm saying this is to alert you to the fact that what you put out to the universe comes back to you—whether wanted or unwanted. You can learn, very easily, how to be more conscious and more deliberate in deciding—note the word "deciding" (this is where you have choice)—what you want to be putting out and attracting to yourself.

Getting back to our harried lives and our inner desires, ask yourself this, "Is there anyone anywhere on the planet who has achieved what I have always dreamed or wanted to achieve?"

The answer to this question is very critical and important for your true success and happiness. Surely if someone else has managed to turn a dream into reality, then you can do it too. That is not a glib answer either! Look at others who are doing what you want to be doing. They're all out there. Whether they are in your state or country, in your city, across the world, or sitting next to you at work, they are out there, and they are the role models you can use to chart your own path.

Ever heard of the word "apprentice"? If it helps, think of yourself that way when it comes to learning about and finally realizing your dream. When you look to others, those who have or are doing similar things to what you want, why not contact one or two of them and ask them how they've managed to do it? I'll bet you dollars to doughnuts you'll get some really great advice and encouragement! All it takes is a little preparation and then action, and before you know it, you'll have your own mentor or mentors helping you.

In fact, that's what our parents, grandparents, business and life coaches, and teachers are to us—mentors. They all help guide us. All we have to do is reach out. That's half the battle right there!

Let me let you in on how the Law of Attraction has worked in my life.

A few years ago, I was living by myself and completely overwhelmed by bills and long-standing debts. I had a decent salary, but the minute I got paid, I had to pay several bills and never had much left over afterward. I was always thinking, "I'll never get ahead. I'm always in debt. The only way up is down." I was always running out of time. I also had a hard time dealing with my boss. This was the lifestyle I had, and my thoughts, feelings, and behaviors followed suit. In short, what I was putting out, I was getting back. Blah!

I felt my life was falling apart.

Whenever I saw people who were successful, I figured they were just lucky. You know, they were born into money, or even if they had to work for it, it was an easy road for them. My difficulties seemed huge in comparison to anything other people go through.

One day, I was with a friend who is really brilliant and seems to have it all, and I asked him, "Why do some people seem to have it all and the rest of us *always* struggle? Is it something we can choose or change?"

My dear friend said, "You know, I have a book by Brian Tracy titled *Create Your Own Future: How to Master the 12 Critical Factors of Unlimited Success.* Why don't you take it home and read it? It should help you find the answer."

That was my first step in exploring the possibilities of how I could have what I wanted in life. I got a lot out of the book, but the big thing that really resonated for me was the idea that if we let others and the circumstances we find ourselves in shape our lives, then we give our power away. I learned you have to be *in charge* of your future, and you have to *make the decisions to make the shift* and make it stick!

It all starts with your thinking. If you think you don't have the power to choose or get what you want, then you are declaring that to the universe. And guess what? That is exactly what you will get. So if you have already chosen to have a limited life, you will attract the people and resources that will bring to you that limited life.

I wanted to know more about this way of thinking, so I sought out information and opportunities to do so. In 2003, I came across Michael Losier's book *Law of Attraction: The Science of Attracting More of What You Want and Less of What You Don't*. I found it straightforward and very simple to understand. What I learned from Losier is if you want something, you'll get it, and conversely, if you *don't* want something, you'll get it!

That's what I'm talking about when I refer to being *conscious* of what you're putting out into the universe. Rather than being subject to the whims of life, with its ever-changing people and situations, like a robot, mindlessly moving from one task to the next, take charge of your thoughts and desires and *create* the path you want to be on—the path of your *wants*!

Therefore, instead of telling yourself, "I'll never make it in this business," replace that negative thought with, "I *will* succeed in my business."

Similarly, change a negative thought from, "All that happens to me is outside my control" to, "I *create* my *own* life and I *will have* happiness and wealth."

Whatever the situation in your life, you can *always* decide to react and act positively. It's your choice.

I started using the Law of Attraction with this basic understanding, and I found amazing results in my career, social life, family, and in every other aspect of my life. I then went further, to see how to enhance my results and how I could best share this with everyone.

Then I made a quantum leap when I discovered the work of Esther and Jerry Hicks (www.abraham-hicks.com). You may know of them through their Law of Attraction—related books or by watching the movie *The Secret*. Another great Law of Attraction resource is Bob Doyle's book *Wealth beyond Reason*.

I am so grateful to have found these and many other teachers of the Law of Attraction. Since using this universal law, I can honestly say my life has changed for the better. I enjoy every single moment as I am designing my life. Yes, I am designing, creating, and living the life I want!

I've gone from living alone and being in financial ruin to having a wonderful wife and children, plus financial freedom. I have been promoted in my job, and I am handling a managerial position as well. My current financial situation allows me to have the money I need to cover all of my bills with more for those extra comforts of life. What seemed impossible in the past has become reality.

I have been so wonderfully moved and inspired by the Law of Attraction and all those who practice it that I have decided to share my teachings with others; to be a mentor, role model, and guide on this incredible life journey. We're all here for a reason, and I know we're also here to help each other. So let me help you in your journey to attracting and having all that you desire.

Remember: The easiest way to make the Law of Attraction work for you is to start paying careful attention to your thoughts. At every moment, you have a choice about what you think. Your thoughts create your reality.

This book has easy and straightforward information on how to use the Law of Attraction. In my first book, *How to Attract Wealth, Health, Love, and Luck into Your Life Immediately*, I covered this subject from a more abstract point of view. You can find my theoretical explanations there.

After explaining the basics of how the Law of Attraction works, we look at the first technique to trigger Law of Attraction: visualization. You will find out that what you visualize is exactly what you attract to yourself! The second technique teaches you about the power of feelings. If you feel happiness, you will attract happiness. The third technique is extremely powerful, and you will soon appreciate its positive impact on your life if you apply it correctly. It is the power of affirmation. The fourth technique is power of meditation, a great multi-purpose, life-enhancing tool. Combine these techniques while using Law of Attraction, and you will be an unstoppable force in your own life! The final section is about goal setting.

It is really amazing how like things attract each other. A person who enjoys a happy life is usually surrounded by happy people. You can easily observe this pattern wherever you look. This pattern is not created by chance; it is created by the Law of Attraction. As you explore the material of this book, you will be able to tap into this powerful law every day, and you will see tremendous results.

The Law of Attraction is working continuously and naturally in shaping your present moment and future life. All you have to do is decide to be conscious and clear about what you want, understand the principles, work with the techniques—

all of which are very easy—and viola, you'll be creating and living the incredible life of which you've always dreamed.

Blessings,

Aiman Al-Maimani

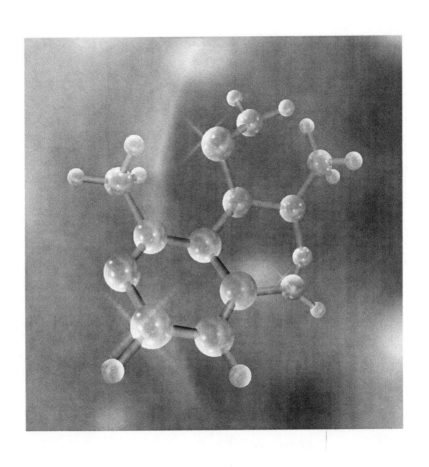

CHAPTER 1

▼

BASIC CONCEPT OF LAW OF ATTRACTION—THE SCIENCE OF HOW IT WORKS

[Success comes in I can, failures in I cannot]

To give you a little background information about the original source of the Law of Attraction, you might need to understand a few facts from quantum physics. Don't worry—you don't need a science degree to understand. It's really very simple!

The Law of Attraction derives its roots from quantum physics; everything in the universe falls into discrete and indivisible units of energy called *quanta*.

The basic component of all material things is energy. Human beings are also energy; our imagination, sounds, feelings, and thoughts are all energies with a specific frequency that correspond to the nature of the item. Furthermore, similar energies (which have similar frequencies) attract each other since they resonate with each other.

This is easily seen by the following example. If you place two pianos in a quiet room, and on one piano, you press the third key from the right, the second piano will absorb the energy on the same key on its own keyboard, and it will resonate and vibrate at the same time. It's amazing how like things attract each other, and this concept is applicable in everything we think of or do!

So, by holding pleasant thoughts and by creating a positive image of success, you will attract more of what you are thinking about, and you will reach and achieve what you desire. On the other hand, by holding bad thoughts about the future, you will resonate with an energy that brings about bad results.

You get what you think. For example, if you think about having a healthier body and you've tried different ways to make yourself healthier, like increasing your physical activity, changing your diet, etc., but you have a limiting belief that you are too old and can't change how your body feels or looks, then you will not end up with a healthy body.

You should eliminate any belief that stops you from creating the right resonance. In this case, for example, you should replace the negative limiting belief with another empowering one like, "Yes, I can be fit and look good at any age! Millions of people keep fit no matter how old they are." These thoughts will help encourage you and keep you in the right mindset to receive all you need to get to your wellness goal.

The Law of Attraction is at work in your life whether you know it or not. No matter what is going on for you, it is a direct result of what the Law of Attraction is absorbing from what you are vibrating (your thought energy). The Law naturally brings you what you're thinking about ... good or bad!

Your reality mirrors your thoughts. To alter or make a change to the image in the mirror, you have to alter your thoughts. It is essential, then, to understand the Law of

Attraction and to use it consciously and deliberately to manifest the "right" reality for you.

Be aware, though, that the Law of Attraction does not differentiate between what you want or don't want. It uses the same rule for everything without exception: similar thoughts and similar energies vibrate, resonate, and connect with each other. In other words, vibrating energy will search the whole universe looking for all similar energies and frequencies. Then both energies will get together and resonate together to form a stronger unity of both. So if you want to experience something, then your wanting (desire) will radiate itself in the universe and similar events, circumstances, and people will be attracted to it (just like a magnet!).

Conversely, if you don't want to experience something, then your un-wanting will radiate itself in the universe searching for similar events, circumstance, and people to resonate with it. This seems like such a simple thing, but if we continue to focus on what we don't want, what we don't want, what we don't want, we will see what we don't want showing up in our lives. If you don't want misery, then you will attract more of it. Make a decision now to choose and focus on what you want. Period.

The first easy step to getting what you want is to be grateful for all that you have. Here again, this sounds so very simple.

Okay, I can do that, you say. But can you? Will you? Are you willing to give conscious energy and effort to be grateful every day for what you have in your life? It is a very simple thing, but it does require *action*. That is a very important thing to remember when it comes to the Law of Attraction. You can follow and understand the principles, but if you don't take action, you will not see results.

You can spend five minutes a day just thinking about all the things you're grateful for; do it at a time that's convenient for you. Or you can write in a journal, tell a friend, meditate, or whatever works for you. As long as you give attention to gratitude, it will make a big difference. This is what starts the Law of Attraction ball rolling.

Every one of us emits light around our bodies. The color of this light corresponds to what we hold in our mind. This field of energy or light around us is also known as the aura. So, your aura will determine what you attract into your experience. This is another way to explain why we attract happy people when we are happy. If we are thinking of something we do not want, our auras will emit that around us, and we will get more of it. If looking at the Law of Attraction from the aura perspective is helpful to improve your understanding of these concepts, I invite you to use it! A great book on the subject is *Aura Advantage: How the Colors in Your Aura Can*

Help You Attain What You Desire and Attract Success, by Cynthia Sue Larson.

Following are some exercises to help you implement these concepts. Law of Attraction teachers like Michal Losier, Esther and Jerry Hicks, and Joe Vitale have all used these exercises in one way or another.

Step One: Declare Your Desire

Get clear about what you want. One way to help you get clear is to list all the things you do and don't want. Yes, even looking at what you don't want will help. It all works to clarify your desires. And feel free to list everything, right down to minute details.

For instance, if you want to get a better position at the company you're in, you may have a list that looks like this:

What I Don't Want
—being stuck doing the same job with no advancement
—staying at the same rate of pay no matter how long I'm there
—putting up with my boss's tirades
—having to work overtime on Fridays

What I Want

—more responsibility
—higher wages
—better communication from my boss
—no overtime

Can you see how the "don't want" list helps you get clear on what you do want? Even though the lists look so similar and easy with regard to writing the opposite of what you don't want, that's the whole idea. This will trigger you to easily change your thoughts accordingly!

Step Two: Trigger It and Vibrate with It

After getting clear about what you want, visualize your desire as if it had already happened. This is extremely powerful. This exercise will help you feel the feelings of having your desire, thereby raising your good vibrations. Make this a consistent thing you do.

Step Three: Maintain It and Allow It

—First you declared your desire.
—Second you visualized yourself having what you want as if it's already manifested—including feeling the feelings, seeing the images, and sensing the sensations of having your desire.
—Now all you have to do to maintain your attraction for what you want is to let it go—and let the universe bring it to

you. Don't get in your own way. Don't get involved in the outcome; just let it go and let it be. Hint: the faster you can let it go out into the vibrational energy field, with good, positive vibrations and gratitude, the faster you will receive!

Chapter One Summary

- The Law of Attraction is based on quantum physics; the basic component of all material things is energy. Human beings are also energy, and similar energies attract each other.

- You get what you think; the Law of Attraction responds to your thoughts and feelings whether conscious or unconscious.

- You can attract what you want, but you first have to get clear, declare your desire, vibrate it, and allow it.

- Visualize your desire as if you already have it.

- Cultivate positive thoughts, be grateful, and watch how your mind opens to possibilities.

CHAPTER 2

▼

VISUALIZE YOUR LIFE THE WAY YOU WANT IT

[Imagine it and you will manifest it]

Visualization is a wonderful technique you can use for getting what you want. It is the fuel that helps run the Law of Attraction in your life. Believe me, you will enjoy amazing results when you begin applying it.

The power of visualization enabled Albert Einstein and all other great inventors to achieve what they imagined. Research has shown that professional athletes use it before going into "the game." Great Law of Attraction teachers use it too! It is a widely used technique that can be applied to all kinds of situations for all kinds of people.

The clearer your vision is, the more precise your result will be. If you dream of owning a red car, visualize a red car, and you will soon be driving that red car. The brain does not differentiate between what is imagined and what is real, so why not aim high and imagine your complete and utter dream life!

Why Visualization Is So Powerful:

In 2001, I was on a trip with my good friend Jack Woolen. We were traveling to California. I've known Jack for about ten years now, and he is always confident and determined about what he wants to achieve, either in his business or personal life.

When Jack and I arranged our trip, we decided to drive rather than fly so we could enjoy the countryside. I was so blessed to have a few hours chatting with him, learning and sharing together. At one point, I turned to Jack and asked him if he had any plans to improve the systems at his job to be more productive and cost-effective.

Jack smiled and said, "Nine months from now, I am going to establish a new company unit to handle all inventory functions for the company sales offices. The new system will be automated. This way, my people will have fewer headaches over manually watching operations."

As he continued describing his plans, I wondered how he would bring this all into place because of all of the things that would need to be done on a practical level like buying the necessary components (computers, hardware, software, etc.) and training people on how to use the new system.

I said, "Well then, in a year from now, you and your team should have a lot of free time if everything's going to be automated."

Jack laughed and said, "Not really!"

"Oh?" I said inquisitively.

"A year from now, I am going to be the head of this department, so I will need to analyze financial data and build strong team leaders, supervisors, and division heads. Lots to do, but my time and my team's time will be used more effectively," Jack said confidently.

I was amazed. "How do you *know* that's where you'll be in a year?"

He said, "You know, I can *see* all of this as if I am already there. I am visualizing the future right now in the present!"

This is the power of visualization. If you can imagine it, you can manifest it.

What Should You Do before Starting the Visualization Process?

It is very important to have a clear goal in mind to be able to manifest it. Once you decide on your goal or desire, then you are ready to start the visualization process to speed up acquiring what you want.

You will need to carve out some time to do this each day, but it doesn't have to take long at all. I promise!

How to Make Visualization Work

Visualization exercises are a great tool, but don't go into exercises thinking, "Oh, this is something I have to do. Goodness, where will I find the time? Who knows if this is going to work?" Remember that in order to change your thinking and behavior, you need to practice—and practice daily. All self-improvement teachers confirm this. New thoughts and behaviors take time to start and maintain. The only way you will maintain this process is to work with it and give it attention every day. Otherwise you can't manifest your desires.

Here Are Some Key Points about Visualization to Keep in Mind:

Do a visualization at least once a day. I understand how hard it is to make the time, so if you can only do this once a day, that's great. However, longer and more frequent periods of visualization create faster results.

Decide which time(s) of the day is best for you.

Come to your visualization already prepared with the goal or desire you want and start feeling the feelings—the confident, knowing feelings—of already having it. The more vivid and clear your goal is and the more confident you are about receiving it, the more accurate your manifestation will be.

Create a visual place to put pictures of your desire or of people you know who already have what you desire. You can create anything for this purpose. You can glue pictures into a book or diary, create a vision board—whatever works for you. This visual aid will work very well to keep you thinking about your goal throughout the day.

You can put your visuals on your bulletin board at work, on your fridge, or on a special wall in your den—anywhere that you will definitely see them during the day. Note: if you create a visual aid for yourself and then keep it hidden, it will be of no use to you. The idea is the more you see what you want, and the more you visualize it and feel it, the more attention you will be giving it. And the Law of Attraction can't help but pick up on what you're doing!

Daily One-Minute to Five-Minutes Visualization Exercise

In this exercise, you will use the power of visualization to speed up your results by guiding the Law of Attraction in the direction you want.

You should do this exercise for about one minute every day at the minimum. It is broken into two parts.

Part One: Sit in a comfortable place. Close your eyes and start to disconnect from the world around you. (Just count backward from fifteen slowly.) This process should take about fifteen seconds.

Part Two: After fifteen seconds, start imagining yourself as if you have already achieved your desire and are enjoying the fine details of it (e.g., see the scene, smell the smells, feel the emotions, etc.). Continue this exercise for forty-five seconds.

This exercise should be done once in the morning and once at night if you can manage it (remember, all you need is a minute or five!). The more you do this, the more you'll notice yourself creating more joyful and positive vibrations that will act as a magnet with the Law of Attraction. Do this exercise consistently in a positive frame of mind, and you'll be amazed at what starts to happen.

Chapter Two Summary

- The power of visualization helps you get closer to your goal. It has worked for famous inventors, top-notch athletes, and numerous Law of Attraction practitioners. It is a simple technique and can be used by anyone.

- The clearer your vision, the more precise your result.

- The brain does not differentiate between what is imagined and what is real.

- It only takes one to five minutes to use visualization every day. Imagine how much more powerful your attracting power will be.

CHAPTER 3

▼

THE MESSENGER WITHIN YOU

The subconscious mind is a powerful entity. It records both the past and present experiences of your life. Like a computer database, your subconscious mind keeps track of what has and what is happening to you. It's like the mind's hard drive—it is what is running in the background while you're automatically operating your software (your conscious mind).

It is from the subconscious mind's database that we form our beliefs, opinions, and primary thought patterns. Whenever you need to make a decision, you search your subconscious archives to check for references to similar situations and outcomes. Together with your "gut instinct," you arrive at the choice you want to make. All sounds good, right? It can be, but it depends on what *type* of thoughts live in your subconscious mind. If you have continual negative and unproductive thoughts that drive your choices, and behaviors—well, I think you already know where I'm going with this—what has shown up in your life is a direct result. The Law of Attraction has responded to those negative thoughts and has matched what you have been vibrating.

But you can change all that! By holding on to lighter, more positive, and focused thoughts about what you want, you basically radiate that frequency into the universe and the Law of Attraction will respond accordingly. The stronger your belief, the faster the result will come to you—as long as you get out of the way of the outcome. Be willing to make the effort to consciously and deliberately use the Law of Attraction principles to achieve your desire. Be clear about what you want. Send out positive feelings and thoughts and let go, knowing—really knowing—that the universe will bring you what you desire. If you have doubts about receiving, you'll either have a delay in getting what you want or it may not come at all.

Focus and Attract

If you focus on prosperity and wealth, then according to the Law of Attraction, you will attract the circumstances, people, and events to give you prosperity and wealth.

If you focus on romance and love, then according to the Law of Attraction, you will attract the circumstances, people, and events that will bring you and romance and love

The Law of Attraction responds to what you focus on. It doesn't matter if you've imagined it, remembered it, or are living it now—in all cases, you will receive what you have focused on.

So What Is Going on in Your Subconscious Mind?

One way to observe what is going on in the subconscious mind is to check your emotions and feelings. If you feel bad, angry, depressed, and so on, that is what the subconscious has or is recording based on the information you're giving it.

There's really nothing wrong with that. It is the way this process naturally works in our bodies and minds. But we can *choose* our thoughts. If you want to stay in negative, unproductive thoughts and emotions, be my guest. However, in order to have better feelings and outcomes, you do need to focus on the thoughts and feelings you want to have instead. Yes, it does mean work—but it's not hard work! You see, our subconscious has been set on a default program most of our lives, which is why we keep repeating the same thoughts and behavior patterns—most of which don't get us where we want to go. But we can change that default setting and make it a brighter, more joyful, and happier one.

Did You Check Your Feel-O-Meter?

Your subconscious mind releases ideas and thoughts into the universe at a certain frequency. Your feel-o-meter, or emotions, will indicate which frequency you are vibrating at.

Are you resonating in alignment with your goal?

Are you picking up the right frequency?

Is your subconscious mind aligned with what you want to create in the universe?

The great thing about the subconscious mind is that it can be reprogrammed any time. So that means we can make a conscious choice to change. All of the great self-improvement leaders have done this. They've modeled for us what we can do for ourselves. We can change our thinking to make change in our lives.

Chapter Three Summary

- The subconscious mind works like the mind's hard drive. And for most of us, it usually runs in negative default mode. But you can replace negative thoughts with positive, freeing, and uplifting thoughts that will create the results you want as you engage the Law of Attraction.

- Focus on what you want. Period. Continually focus on what you want in order to attract it.

- Check your emotions and feelings. These not only help you see what you're attracting but also help you understand what you're "feeding" your subconscious.

- Learn to reprogram your subconscious mind, and you can change your life.

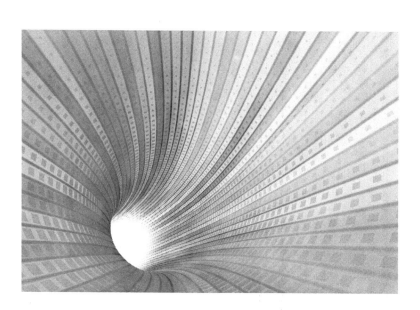

CHAPTER 4

▼

THE POWER OF AFFIRMATION

[Whisper in the ear of the universe and watch the magic]

As you have been learning, if you put out what you want to the universe it will come to you. So if you want to manifest what you desire and see magic happen, then whisper in the ear of the universe with your most positive, joyful, and grateful thoughts, and watch what unfolds.

All of us have dreams inside of us—those things that call to us to remind us we haven't yet arrived at our potential or our ultimate calling. The Law of Attraction can help us get to where we want to be—it's happened again and again for countless people, and it can happen for you, too.

Along with getting clear about what you want, visualizing it, and letting it go, another effective tool that will help in this process is using affirmations.

What Is an Affirmation?

An affirmation is a word or phrase you say repeatedly to yourself on any subject or thought. In this case, I only want you to use positive affirmations!

Why Are Affirmations Effective?

The subconscious mind is programmed by repetitive thoughts, images, and associated feelings. Up until now, you have probably been running on your default mode—having negative and stressful repetitive thoughts that drive your decisions and behaviors. Here's your chance to change old and unproductive thought patterns by consciously using positive affirmations.

Examples of Powerful Affirmations You Can Use on a Daily Basis:

• I love my job and looking forward to getting to the office every day.

• I am a lovable and joyful person.

• I love knowing I inspire people.

Design Your Own Affirmations and Try This Twenty-One-Day Exercise:

Your thoughts and images should be in sync with your goals and life vision. This exercise helps you with the consistency you need to keep achieve your goal. It's not hard. It, like everything else you've been learning, just takes practice. Remember, we are using our conscious mind to *deliberately* attract what we want.

Once you have established some powerful affirmations, do the following:

1. Write them down twenty-one times for twenty-one days.

2. Repeat every morning, noon, and evening until your goal arrives—and it will!

Components of a Good Affirmation Statement:

Your statement in either case should have the following characteristics:

Keep It Short for Easy Recall:

Keeping your affirmation short will make it easy to remember, so instead of saying, "I am enjoying a wonderful relationship with my wife, Julia, my son, Brad, and my daughter, Anna," you might say, "I am enjoying a happy relationship with my family."

Be Specific:

If you affirm your goal with specific details, you will get specific results. If your affirmations are vague or mixed, your results will be vague or mixed.

Instead of saying, "I am enjoying driving my Lexus now," you might say, "I am enjoying driving my golden Lexus now."

Keep the Present Tense in Your Statement:

This is the part you should never miss. Always keep the present tense in your affirmations. Otherwise you will be giving out the wrong message to the universe. Do not expect your happiness to come later, because later will always be later!

Instead of saying, "I will enjoy my family life once I build my business," you can say, "I am enjoying life with my family."

Your Statement Must Be Empowering:

If your statement is weak, it will not create the right emotion or feeling. Emotions are the fuel for your creative power to attract what you want. Words like "I will try" or "I will do my best" or "at least" or "I might" are not powerful like "I am."

Instead of saying, "I will try to build my own business as soon as possible," you can say, "I am building my business every day."

Use "Ing" If You Can:

Use "ing" to embellish the effect of your affirmation. Use the right words and the right tense.

Instead of saying, "I enjoy loving my wife," you can say, "I am enjoying loving my wife."

Repeat Every Morning and Every Evening:

You need to affirm what you want every morning and every evening at a minimum, as repetition is how you will make changes. However, I found it very useful to do this three times as mentioned by R. H. Jarrett in the book titled *It Works*. This will help you not only to change your thinking but also to get faster results.

Some Hints and Clues for Effective Repetitions:

- Write your statement down.

- Keep a small note or card in your wallet.

- Read your small card multiple times every day.

Use Images or Pieces from Journals, Newspapers, Etc:

This will work for you as a visual affirmation. Keep a few clippings of newspaper stories or articles of your dream home or dream car, etc. This helps remind you of your desires, and each time you think about or look at these images, you will be sending out good feelings and thoughts that the Law of Attraction will respond to.

Be Innovative in Your Affirmation:

Create a symbol to remind you of your desire. Like a rubber band on your wrist, you can use this symbol to prompt an image in your mind. If your symbol is a tree with green leaves, then draw your symbol on a piece of paper and stick it in your office, home, car, etc. Notice all the trees with green leaves on your way to work! You can also use a symbol you hear—for instance, birds singing or people laughing. Every time you see or hear your symbol, you affirm your goal again.

Chapter Four Summary

- Affirmations are strong and powerful words or statements you say or write over and over again to stay focused on your desire.

- Keep affirming statements short, specific, and in the present tense.

- Use newspaper or article clippings as a visual affirmation of your desire.

- Create a symbol of your affirmation. A symbol could be visual or auditory. Each time you see or hear your symbol, you will be reminded of your desire.

CHAPTER 5

▼

MEDITATE IN NATURE

[Time for your mind to fly]

Each day, from the moment you open your eyes until you finally fall into peaceful slumber (I hope!), your brain is overloaded. Whether you're having what you think is a relatively calm and predictable day or you're in the throes of a frazzled maze of appointments and deadlines, your brain is being taxed.

Sleep is important, not only for rest and healing but also because it gives the brain its due "space" to relax and rejuvenate. You know what it's like to wake up refreshed and alert. So that's the feeling you want to expand on and repeat as often as you can. It stands to reason that the more you can be "quiet" and let your brain have a rest, the more you'll benefit.

Is there a "mechanism" you can use do that? Definitely! And the best part is that you can use this mechanism while you are awake.

This "mechanism" is called meditation. Meditation is a technique that utilizes the power of the subconscious mind in creating what you want in life. Albert Einstein approximated that we only use less than 10 percent of our mental power. By practicing meditation, you will have access to the other 90 percent.

People often practice meditation to reclaim their inner peace or to go within to commune with their source energy. Here, I want you to use meditation for activating the Law of Attraction and to access your subconscious mind to plant the seed for controlling your thoughts.

Throughout your meditation, it is important to keep your thoughts and images positive and beautiful.

How Often Should You Meditate?

It is great if you can do this for twenty to thirty minutes on a daily basis. It is recommended to pick a convenient but regular time of day for practice. For me, I like to end my day by sitting quietly, reading an uplifting verse, and talking over my day with my source of wisdom and comfort.

It is your choice to pick an appropriate meditation in accordance with your personal wellness goals and the Law of Attraction. The point I'm making is to find a way to do this for at least twenty to thirty minutes a day. Making the time to do this will build both consistency and lasting benefits.

I recommend starting by looking for good scripts for meditations and then recording one you like on a tape. Just make sure to read it yourself, with a soft and empowering voice. Be very imaginative and keep good diction and pace as you read. If you can, time it for twenty to thirty minutes (as I mentioned before); that is best. As your meditation skills grow, you can increase time beyond thirty minutes.

It's important that you set up a place that is very quiet for you without any distractions. Close your eyes, and put your top three goals in mind.

Here is an example of a meditation script:

Say to yourself, "I am attracting all that I want now."

Start to focus on your breath. Take three very gentle and deep breaths. With each inhalation, imagine the whole universe giving you all the energy, luck, resources, and courage you need to achieve your goal. With each exhalation, release all fears, limitations, and obstacles that stand against your goal.

Now imagine you see a green field with three big trees, and each one of the trees has been put there to support one of your three goals.

Each tree has colorful branches with all kind of fruits. Those fruits are really the resources that you need to achieve your goal.

Birds are scattered on and around the trees. They are singing to confirm to you that you are receiving your goal now. They are singing with a beautiful sound to assure you that they can see your vision and your dreams coming true.

Look at the first tree. Do you see the flowers embracing the base of the tree? It is really fantastic to come close and touch the flowers and hear the birds singing, "Your dream has come true."

You are extremely happy. Your smile is very wide and you "see" your eyes shining as they embrace this wonderful feeling.

You know and accept that the whole universe is supporting you completely. Your first goal has been reached.

As you look around, a soft breeze touches your skin, and you see the second tree with hundreds of beautiful roses surrounding it. A compelling scent shifts your attention now to walk toward those roses. You touch one of those roses as you stand tall and proud of your achievement of the second goal. The birds are crooning and woodpeckers are carving your achievement on the second tree. What a wonderful feeling you have now. You are asking and receiving what you want.

Now you can't wait to discover the third tree. The third tree is moving toward you this time. You've been waiting for this to come to you, and it is walking to you. You are, in fact, surrounded by a colorful shadow from the three trees. It is like a circle around you. Your body is touched by the different kind of flowers and roses. You can smell the nice fresh air filling your life.

Now, you want to enjoy these moments by letting your mind be free of any thought and just feeling your happiness.

Note: Keep a period of five to ten minutes in your recording as silence. No script at all should be read here.

Celebrate these moments and accept all the universal energy to achieve anything in this life. Whatever goal you have, you can achieve it. Know it, feel it, and believe it.

Now focus again on your breath.

Breathe gently and deeply three times. With each inhalation, imagine the whole universe is giving you all the energy, luck, resources, and courage you need to achieve anything you want. With each exhalation, release all fears, limitations, and obstacles that stand in your way.

Open your eyes, and massage your hands together. Massage your face.

Well done!

As you practice doing meditation, you will find a script that you really enjoy. Use it or change it as often as you like.

I have found the following points helpful in practicing mediation:

- Imagine every cell in your head, body, arms, hands, legs, and so on is deeply relaxed.

- Breathe slowly and deeply as much as possible at the beginning and end of your mediation.

- Ask the creator of the universe to help you get what you want.

- Give your mind a chance to fly with only positive pictures and empowering images.

- Do not limit your dreams. Dream as big as possible; it does not cost you more.

- Build patience through silence in your mediation. I assure you that in silence you can "hear" what is needed.

- Know yourself much deeper, as you "sit" with yourself again and again.

Chapter Five Summary

• Meditation connects you with the power of your subconscious mind and your higher self.

• Meditation slows you down, takes you out of overload, and lets your mind rest. When the mind is resting, it's in its most creative state.

• As you meditate, include the power of affirmation and visualization.

• Meditate twenty to thirty minutes on a daily basis. Additional time spent meditating stimulates more of your mind's creative force and quickens the manifestation of desires.

CHAPTER 6

▼

THE POWER OF EXPECTATION

[If you can expect it, you can get it]

Successful people expect to be successful. Period. Conversely, people who fail expect to fail.

During my university days, I had a friend who always expected to get an A in his courses. And accordingly, he did. I took that lesson and applied it myself and found I was more motivated and dedicated to doing the work and eventually, I achieved what I expected. And the same has held true for me in my career.

The power of your expectation depends on your perception of the universe. By changing your perception of who you are, you can change your reality. Your expectations are a thought process that transmits messages into the universe at a certain frequency. The universe will respond by manifesting what you've expected. Expect something great, and it will appear. Expect something so-so, and it will also appear.

If you are expecting to have something, then you have to be confident and deliberate about getting it. If you want to achieve wealth or health, etc., you need to build your expectation toward that. Then the Law of Attraction will attract the resources, circumstances, and right people to bring you what you expected.

You might ask, "How long does the Law of Attraction take to bring me what I want?"

I would reply, "That depends entirely on how much you keep your thoughts on what you want!"

All you have to do is:

- think the thoughts

- feel the feelings

- expect what you want with confidence

- let it go

And the universe will do the rest.

Chapter Six Summary

- Your expectations are a thought process that transmits messages into the universe at a certain frequency.

- Expect to be successful and you will be.

- Be confident in your expectations (i.e., remove doubt).

- Keep all thoughts and feelings about your desire positive and expect excellent results!

CHAPTER 7

▼

GOALS HANDBOOK

Set your goals and determine what you really want
[Rest your ladder on the right wall]

In a football game, all players have one objective in mind: to win.

The game has certain rules that govern each movement. It has a start time, duration, and end time. Smart strategies are needed to win the game, and this necessitates a coach or trainer who works as a mentor with the players. It requires a lot of cooperation, determination, and a firm commitment from each player to achieve the victory.

The strategies and effort applied to achieving the goal of winning a football game applies to life.

The Basic Model of Setting Goals

The very basic model for goal setting consists of the following main elements:

1. Goal Determination and Listing (Also Known As Clarity of Goal)

2. Goal Filtration

3. Goal Prioritizing

4. Goal Implementation and Strategy

5. Goal Achievement and Appreciation

1. Goal Determination and Listing (Also Known As Clarity of Goal):

The first step in achieving and attracting your desires is to determine clearly and vividly what your goals are. Write down your dreams and wishes for today and the future. Even write down your past and current achievements—anything that raises your good thoughts and feelings while working toward your next set of goals. By using your past achievements and dreams for the future, you can be really specific about what you want to achieve now.

What If I Do Not Know What I Want?

I have found the following a useful technique to help you get clear on what you want. Don't be daunted by asking yourself seventy questions. You'll find once you start formulating the questions, you'll see a theme or pattern that will help you get clarity.

Step 1: Ask Yourself At Least Seventy Questions

Ask yourself every possible question for what do you want in this life today and in the future.

This is known as a discovery process. Questions might be anything, such as what could you do to have better health? What could you do to create more friends? How can you improve your work? What can you do better to take care of yourself? And so on.

The idea is not to limit yourself, as this process will open new avenues or hidden goals. You might run out of questions after thirty or so. That's okay. Keep going. Dig deeper inside to reach what you really want.

Step 2: Formulate in Each Category Your Goals

Let's say, for example, that you found twenty questions concerning your health. You know now that health is a major category. You might find your goals for health are playing squash three times a week, eating more vegetables, and getting more rest. There you go; you've created three clear goals out of those twenty questions!

2. Goal Filtration

Group similar goals together and come up with a shorter, more focused list. List what you see is comfortable and manageable for you. Next list what you think is impossible to do now. This will eliminate putting effort into directions that won't move you forward today.

Some goals might be marked as impossible now, since you might need to achieve other goals to prepare you for them. Let's say you want to establish a million-dollar business, but you are in debt right now. This may be impossible now; however, you can take steps toward it first by getting out of debt and then by developing your business every day.

As you work toward your goals, determine what you need to do, know, or have to get them. For example, say you want to develop public-speaking skills. What's the first thing you need to do? Perhaps you should sign up for a night school course or study individually with a voice coach. Next you could practice speaking in front of friends or co-workers. Next you could make a speech at your neighborhood center, etc. You see the picture I'm creating here.

3. Goal Prioritization: I Have So Much to Do. Where to Start?

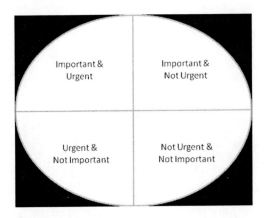

Take your original list of goals and categorize them into the four groups as shown in the model above. Then do the following:

• Create a card or a sheet for each discipline with the four-quadrant method.

• Make multiple sheets; each one of them will list the four quadrants.

• Create your master plan.

By using the four-quadrant model, you can easily decide which goals in which grouping should be focused on first.

The problem most people have lies within quadrant two, the important but not urgent. The reason they have a problem is because the important but not urgent gets submerged under what is important and urgent at the same time. This is usually a result of poor planning. When you plan your goals ahead of time, you will avoid urgency as much as possible and thus you will create a stronger focus in your life.

4. Goal Implementation and Strategy

Use mind-mapping techniques to nail down everything associated with your goals. Then create a detailed plan for your top ten goals. Next, create a document to track goals.

Use the following as boosters

- Visualization (see Chapter Two)

- Feeling (see Chapter Three)

- Affirmation (see Chapter Four)

- Meditation (see Chapter Five)

Another great way to help boost you as you work on your goals is to find a mentor or coach who will help you stay on track. It's especially good if you can find a mentor who already has the goal you are seeking. This will further motivate you to achieve it.

5. Goal Achievement and Appreciation

Once you've achieved your goal, you can be sure you will continue attracting success. Success attracts more success. It is always important to track your progress and lessons learned along the way. And document and celebrate all successes, whether big or small!

Track Your Progress

Once you've decided on a goal, you'll need to keep a journal or log to track your progress. Along the way, you'll be making decisions that will impact the direction you'll go in. Create a timeline. For example, say you want to lose twenty pounds in six months. So if you start your goal on May 1, your timeline takes you to November 1. During that time, record your progress—the ups, the downs, and everything in between!

Document Lessons Learned

Your aim from this exercise is to detect your pattern of reactions whenever you are working toward a goal. You'll know how you're doing by watching what shows up in your life. You will see that failure contributes to more failure if you allow your thoughts to go there. Similarly, you will find that your success contributes to more success. By documenting the process of reaching your goal, you will have a written road map that will help you see the whole experience from start to finish. Good job!

Celebrate Your Achievements

In order to keep yourself motivated and on track, you need to acknowledge, appreciate, and have gratitude for every small or large achievement you make along the way. Using the above example, if, say, by June 15, you have lost five pounds, you will write down the achievement in your journal or log, but also reward yourself mentally by being grateful and proud that you have done it. The more good feelings and thoughts you have while working toward your goal, the more you will help make it happen!

Chapter Seven Summary

- Set your goals and determine what you really want.

- If you're not entirely clear about what you want, ask yourself seventy questions. Then use the four-quadrant chart to organize your goals into groups and priorities.

- Use mind-mapping techniques to nail down everything associated with your goals. Then create a detailed plan for your top ten goals.

- Track your progress and lessons learned along the way.

- Celebrate all of your achievements, big or small.

Exercise
Twenty-One-Day Exercise for Affirming Your Most Important Goals

[Think it, write it, and watch the wonder]

This is a wonderful twenty-one-day program I would like you to do with your most important goals. I mentioned this exercise in my book titled *How to Attract Wealth, Health, Love, and Luck into Your life Immediately: A Concise Manual for Personal Success.*

I will describe this program in detail, and I want you to observe the use of visualization and emotions in weeks two and three respectively. Be sure to have a journal or notebook handy for this as well.

The Law of Attraction brings your thoughts and goals together, therefore what shows up in your life and what you feel is what you think about most. This exercise can help make you think about resources, ideas, and shortcuts to get to your goal very quickly. It will attract similar energies to vibrate with your thoughts and actions.

The procedure has been broken into the following three steps. Each step has to be completed within a certain period of time. Furthermore, each step has one exercise that will be described in detail.

To really make this process work, you must commit to follow the three steps according to the schedule as outlined.

Step One—Starts Day One (see below for actual exercise)

This first step starts on the first day and continues for twenty-one days. You need to complete Exercise One on a daily basis during the twenty-one days.

Step Two—Starts Day Eight (see below for actual exercise)

The second step begins on day eight of the twenty-one days and continues daily through the twenty-one days. You need to complete Exercise Two on a daily basis during the rest of the twenty-one days.

Step Three—Starts Day Fifteen (see below for actual exercise)

The last step starts on day fifteen and continues daily to the end of the program. You need to complete Exercise Three on a daily basis during the remainder of the twenty-one days.

Your success in activating the Law of Attraction depends heavily on your commitment to completing the three steps without missing a day. I know how easy it is to procrastinate, but please don't. The process simply won't work unless you do it as instructed. It is guaranteed to have a tremendous effect on achieving your goals in a way that you have never dreamed of.

A Very Important Note to Keep In Mind

Tell no one about your program while you work on it. You can only inform others after you achieve your goal. This helps keep your concentration crystal clear as some people might distract you or discourage you, and this will work against you. So keeping quiet is essential for the success of the three different steps and the three exercises.

Step One

You will do this exercise for twenty-one days. It is broken into two parts.

Exercise One—Part A

Write your goal in a clear, short, and powerful statement as if you have already achieved it.

If your goal is to attract something like having a closer relationship with your partner, then your statement could be, "I have a wonderful and loving relationship with my partner now."

If your goal is to acquire a certain amount of money, then your statement could be, "I have $100,000.00 in my account now."

For a career goal, your statement could be, "I am an expert in computer networking technology," "I am the head of my department now," or "I am an outstanding employee now."

On the other hand, if your goal is to repel something, like weight reduction, then you need to make your statement sound positive.

You could write, "I have a fit and healthy body now."

Or if your goal were to quit smoking, you would write, "I am enjoying deep breathing and excellent health now."

Exercise One—Part B

Take out your trusty journal or notebook (one that has at least twenty-one days of pages in it). Now that you have written your goal in a clear, short, and powerful statement, each day for the next three weeks, you will write the page number, the date, and then write your statement twenty-one times on the page.

Step Two

You should have completed Exercise One during your first week, and you should be continuing it as you move into Step Two. In this exercise, I will move you through the tunnel experience we covered earlier. This exercise will take one minute every day. It is broken into two parts as well.

Exercise Two—Part A (Establishing the Tunnel Experience)

Do this exercise every morning. Sit in a comfortable place. First, close your eyes and start to disconnect from the world around you. (Just count backward from fifteen slowly.) This process should take about fifteen seconds.

Exercise Two—Part B

After fifteen seconds, start imagining yourself as if you have already achieved your goal, and imagine you are enjoying the fine details of it (e.g., the smell, color, touch, emotions). Continue this exercise for forty-five seconds.

Continue this daily throughout the rest of the program. This exercise helps reduce the distance between your thoughts and your goals. You will see an amazing improvement toward getting your goal in hands.

Remember you are still working with Exercise One as you incorporate Exercise Two.

Step Three

You have been working with Exercises One and Two. Exercise Three covers days fifteen to twenty-one.

Exercise Three—Part A (Goal Achievement Appreciation)

In this exercise, you become part of the Law of Attraction function. You need to recognize and appreciate every small and large sign toward your goal achievement. This exercise takes one minute every night. It is broken into two parts.

Once you are at home and before you go to bed, start the tunnel experience with Exercise Two but without going into your thoughts. First, close your eyes and start the connection part (count backward from fifteen slowly). This process should take about fifteen seconds.

Exercise Three—Part B

Start to appreciate any small or large step toward your goal, and then follow that by imagining that you have already achieved your goal with its details. Do this for forty-five seconds. You will do this exercise on a daily basis during the third week of this program as well as continuing with Exercises One and Two.

References and Recommended Readings

Al-Maimani, Aiman A., 2006. *How to Attract Wealth, Health, Love, and Luck into Your Life Immediately: A Concise Manual for Personal Success.* Lincoln, NE: iUniverse.

Begley, Sharon, 2007. *Train Your Mind, Change Your Brain: How a New Science Reveals Our Extraordinary Potential to Transform Ourselves.* Ballantine Books.

Byrne, Rhonda, 2006. *The Secret.* Atria Books/Beyond Words.

Byrne, Rhonda, 2006. *The Secret* (Extended Edition) DVD. TS Production, LLC.

Canfield, Jack, 2000. *The Power of Focus: How to Hit Your Business, Personal and Financial Targets with Absolute Certainty.* HCI.

Canfield, Jack, 2006. *The Success Principles: How to Get From Where You Are to Where You Want to Be.* Collins.

Canfield, Jack and D.D. Watkins, 2007, *Jack Canfield's Key to Living the Law of Attraction: A Simple Guide to Creating the Life of Your Dreams.* HCI.

Doyle, Bob, 2006. *Wealth beyond Reason.* Trafford Publishing.

Eker, T. Harv, 2005. *Secrets of the Millionaire Mind: Mastering the Inner Game of Wealth.* Collins.

Evers, Anne Marie, 1999. *Affirmations Your Passport to Happiness.* Berkana Books.

Evers, Anne Marie, and Christine Einarson, 2003. *Affirmations Your Passport to Prosperity/Money.* Affirmations-International Publishing.

Evers, Anne Marie, and Laurel von Pander, 2002. *Affirmations Your Passport to Lasting, Loving Relationships.* Affirmations-International Publishing.

Gawain, Shakti, 2003. *Create Your Own Affirmations: A Creative Visualization Kit.* New World Library.

Hay, Louise, 2005. *The Power of Your Spoken Word* (Audio CD). Hay House.

Hay, Louise, 2007. *The Present Moment: 365 Daily Affirmations.* Hay House.

Hicks, Esther, and Jerry Hicks, 2007. *The Astonishing Power of Emotions.* Hay House.

Hicks, Esther, and Jerry Hicks, 2006. *The Law of Attraction: The Basics of the Teachings of Abraham.* Hay House.

Hicks, Esther, Jerry Hicks, and Wayne W. Dyer, 2004. *Ask and It Is Given: Learning to Manifest Your Desires.* Hay House.

Jarrett, R. H., 1976. *It Works.* DeVorss & Company.

Jarrett, R. H., and James Allen, 2007. *It Works AND As a Man Thinketh.* www.bnpublishing.com.

Larson, Cynthia Sue, 2006. *Aura Advantage: How the Colors in Your Aura Can Help You Attain What You Desire and Attract Success.* Lightworker Publishing.

Lin, Chunyi, and Gary Rebstock, 2006. *Born A Healer: I was born a healer. You were born a healer, too!.* Spring Forest Qigong Company, Inc.

Losier, Michael J., 2007. *Law of Attraction: The Science of Attracting More of What You Want and Less of What You Don't.* Wellness Central.

Mohr, Barbel, 2001. *The Cosmic Ordering Service.* Hampton Roads Publishing Company.

Mohr, Barbel and Dawn Bailiff (Translator), 2007. *Cosmic Ordering: The Next Adventure.* Hampton Roads Publishing Company.

Murphy, Joseph, 2008. *The Power of Your Subconscious Mind.* Wilder Publications.

Peale, Norman Vincent, 2007. *The Power of Positive Thinking.* Fireside.

Peale, Norman Vincent, 1996. *Positive Imaging: The Powerful Way to Change Your Life.* Ballantine Books.

Ray, James Arthur, 1999. *The Science of Success: How to Attract Prosperity and Create Harmonic Wealth Through Proven Principles.* Sun Ark Press.

Ray, James Arthur, 2008. *HARMONIC WEALTH: THE SECRET OF ATTRACTING THE LIFE YOU WANT.* Hyperion.

Robbins, Anthony, 2001. *Unlimited Power: The New Science Of Personal Achievement.* Pocket Books.

Taylor, Sandra Anne, 2006. *Quantum Success: The Astounding Science of Wealth and Happiness.* Hay House.

Taylor, Sandra Anne, 2001. *Secrets of Attraction: The Universal Laws of Love, Sex and Romance.* Hay House.

Tracy, Brian, 2005. *Create Your Own Future: How to Master the 12 Critical Factors of Unlimited Success.* Wiley.

Tracy, Brian, 2006. *Getting Rich Your Own Way: Achieve All Your Financial Goals Faster Than You Ever Thought Possible.* Wiley.

Tracy, Brian, 2004. *Goals! How to Get Everything You Want—Faster Than You Ever Thought Possible.* Berrett-Koehler Publishers.

Vitale, Joe, 2006. *The Attractor Factor: 5 Easy Steps for Creating Wealth (or Anything Else) from the Inside Out.* Wiley.

Vitale, Joe, 2007. *The Key: The Missing Secret for Attracting Anything You Want.* Wiley.

Wilde, Stuart, 1995. *Affirmations.* Hay House.

Index

Webpage Address for This Book
http://www.lawofattractionhandbook.com

978-0-595-42974-5
0-595-42974-2

Printed in the United Kingdom
by Lightning Source UK Ltd.
136218UK00001B/92/P